Freedom
A Southern Girl's Truth

FREEDOM

A Southern Girl's Truth

Poetry by Tonya Crawford Baldwin

Copyright © 2018 Tonya Crawford Baldwin

Book Cover Design by Ina Hamburg

Author Photo by Jaquan Crawford

Book Design by Tonya Crawford Baldwin

Published by Completely Novel

All rights reserved. This book is protected by the copyright laws of the United States of America. No part of this book may be reproduced, stored in a retrieval system, or transmitted in any form or by any means, without the written permission of the author.

ISBN: 9781787233126

Printed in the United States of America

DEDICATION

This book is dedicated to:

My grandparents Catherine and Hardie J. Rivers, the foundation of our family. I love and miss you dearly.

My dear cousin Alicia McCluney, who had a heart of gold and the prettiest smile in the world.

My cousin Shatina Rivers, who was an absolute sweetheart, not only beautiful on the outside, but on the inside as well.

Rest in peace......until we meet again angels.

ACKNOWLEDGEMENTS

I would like to acknowledge my family and friends. Thank you all for encouraging me to share my creative energy with the world through poetry. I extend a special thank you to my wonderful and supportive husband Robert and to our five boys, you make my heart smile. Much love to my mom Josephine. I strive to be more like you every day; kind-hearted, strong-willed and beautiful. I'm thankful for my dad Casey, your baby girl finally did it! I am grateful for the love from my siblings KC and Shareka. I appreciate all the support from my extended family and friends. I love you all dearly. Most importantly, I give the ultimate praise and thanks to God. Thank you for your grace and for allowing me to share my gift with the world.

TABLE OF CONTENTS

Introduction ... 8

Freedom to Live ... 12

Little Brown Girl ... 17

Miss Me in 2016 ... 19

In a Bottle ... 24

Two Hearts One Soul ... 28

I Wear the "S" ... 30

Life Happened ... 32

Gem ... 33

Karma ... 35

Don't Cry for Me ... 37

Dope Love ... 39

Grandma's Biscuits ... 40

Soar Red Bird Soar ... 44

Joy ... 45

Soul Dance ... 46

But God... ... 49

The Grass ... 51

Stand in Your Truth ... 53

About The Author ... 54

INTRODUCTION

Freedom, A Southern Girl's Truth, is dear to my heart. Writing this book brought revelation, spiritual growth, and a closer connection with my inner-being. I pray that you find familiarity in my writings, relatable moments, and realize that we all deal with the uncertainties of life's ups and downs. It is my hope that I can inspire you to, embrace differences, push through storms, forgive those who have wronged you, celebrate successes and learn to love yourself just the way you are. There is freedom in self-love and living in your truth. It's a journey, but one worth taking!

Jaquan and Josiah I love you beyond the moon! Know that your happiness comes from self-love. Self-love must be accomplished before you begin to love others. Also, know that you can do anything that you put your minds to. No one holds you back from your dreams more than self. You have a choice, so choose you! Don't forget to thank those who helped you along the way.
– Mom

"Loving me is what set me free!"

Tonya Crawford Baldwin

Stand fast therefore in the liberty wherewith Christ hath made us free, and be not entangled again with the yoke of bondage.
Galatians 5:1 (KJV)

Freedom to Live

Freedom is

To love

To have a voice

To be heard

To give

To those who are less fortunate

To be happy in a world full of chaos

To forgive and forget

To laugh out loud

To dance in the clouds

To spread your wings

To have hopes and dreams

To explore your talents

To stand up for what you believe in

To agree to disagree or

To remain silent

To pick your battles

To be at peace

To have joy

Freedom is knowing

That you have the choice

To live

14

"It takes a whole village to raise a single child"- Yoruba Proverbs

(Tonya at one year old, picture courtesy of mom)

Little Brown Girl

Little brown girl hold your head up high

You are simply beautiful

One can't deny

Golden honey coils

A crown of perfection

Lovely smile

Radiant bronze complexion

Your melanin is glistening

As if kissed by the sun

Be yourself and have loads of fun

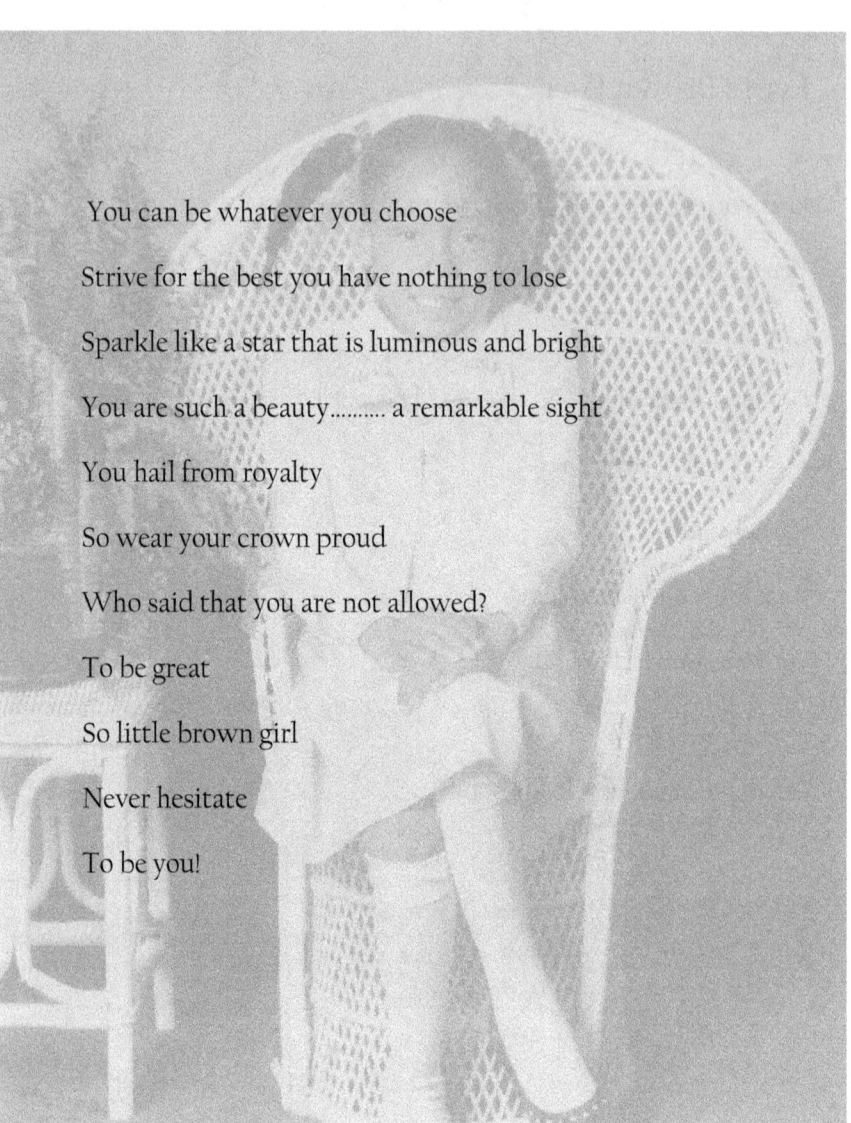

You can be whatever you choose

Strive for the best you have nothing to lose

Sparkle like a star that is luminous and bright

You are such a beauty.......... a remarkable sight

You hail from royalty

So wear your crown proud

Who said that you are not allowed?

To be great

So little brown girl

Never hesitate

To be you!

(Little Brown Girl, Tonya)

Miss Me in 2016

Miss me in 2016

Looking forward to another year and all that it brings

Leaving the baggage of the past behind

Embracing what's to come

What is for me is mine

Miss me in 2016

A year of crazy debates

A world divided of

People filled with hate

Senseless deaths of the young and old

Merely existing in a place that's cold

Saying my goodbyes ready to greet the new

Opportunities for change that are far and few

No regrets, taking the good with the bad

Holding on to hopes that I once had

To make a difference in a world

Where possibilities are endless

Searching for ways to continue to bless

Those who have lost their way

It is a new year and a new day

So Miss me in 2016

(My 40th birthday photo shoot, picture courtesy of Jaquan)

A Change is Gonna Come-Sam Cooke

In a Bottle

I wish I could take "prejudice"

Put it in a bottle and toss it in the ocean

Watch it in motion

All of the ugliness, stupidity, hate, ignorance and animosity

Let "shame on you" follow all of its days

Pour in the "hurt" that it causes as it floats away

Into a sea of forgetfulness....ready for the day

When people are judged no more

As it washes up on shore

Only to be tossed over and over again

Until it sinks in

That bigotry has to stop

Killing us slowly drowning in our sorrows

Wondering and praying for a new tomorrow

One without doubt, fear, bias, negativity, discrimination

Put "prejudice" in a bottle

As it travels all over the nation

Let it reach the hearts of many

In hopes that it will be buried deep

Never to be recovered again

"A song fluttered down in the form of a dove, and it bore me a message, the one word-Love!" -**Paul Laurence Dunbar**

Two Hearts One Soul
(for my husband Robert)

I was in a place that I never knew existed

A dream, a mere thought....

You were a hope I buried inside deep

Longing for a whisper

Destiny was awakened by sweet sounds of love

Lit a fire and caressed a heart that was broken, shattered and torn

On a Planet far above

You are my love

Two hearts one soul

When no one else was there

I knew you would care

Two hearts one soul

Patient, encouraging and kind

Qualities that are hard to find

Two hearts one soul

Can't fathom being a part

You will always have my heart

You are my soul

To have and to hold

Two hearts one soul

Will love you until my last breath

Nothing separating us but death

We will forever be bound

Tied together

Never broken

These are the words

God has spoken

Two hearts one soul

I Wear the "S"

Underneath it all

Unrobed and unclothed

I am unbothered because I wear the "S"

The "S" is for

Shattered but not broken

Scorned but not scarred

I slipped but didn't fall

And through it all

I remained solid

Wrapped in pain

My heart stayed the same

Sincere

The "S" represents strength in my weakest moments

Sweet victory over my opponents

I smile.... knowing all the while

I wear the "S"

A survivor of my circumstances

Blessed by a savior of second chances

I am at peace....

So many nights I cried

A little part of me died

But I am free....

Free to be smart, successful and superb

A better me

Self-Confident, self-loved and spirit-filled

And because of the life He gave

I am forever saved...

I wear the "S"

Life Happened

Tick tock is the sound of time travel

Grasping on to every second

I've arrived but I'm unaware

Of how I got here

No turning back the hands

Time has moved on

It's written in stone

Life Happened...............

Gem
(for my first-born Jaquan)

Who would have thought?

In an instance my life would change

Elevated to greater heights unimaginable

You were born and I was torn

Up until that moment

I struggled with what I thought love to be

Round face brown eyes looking up at me

You were a sight to behold

Pure as sugar cane

Sprouting from my very being

On this day I found happiness

A piece of my soul shaped and molded

A GEM for all to see

Chiseled

Entrusted in my hands

A mere gift from my creator

The epitome of perfection

A transparent reflection

Of my Heart ♡

Karma

Some say that fate is contingent on your actions

With this knowledge at hand

Why is it so hard for many to understand?

Karma

What you sow....you shall reap

Not to get to deep but..........

I want my harvest to be bountiful

Overflowing with blessing unmeasurable

I want to wake up each day to make a difference

To be the change I would like to see

There is no other way for me

The Golden Rule is to…….

"Treat others how you want to be treated"

So don't be a fool

Karma is your awaited destiny

Are you blind and can't see?

The hate that you spew

With emptiness deep within you

Deliberately bringing others down

Constantly meeting smiles with a frown

Scheming and plotting while in disguise

It's only until your demise

That you realize

It's Karma

Don't Cry for Me

(dedicated to my dear cousins RIP)

Sitting by his throne

The Lord called me home

Don't cry for me I'm with my Father

Pearly Gates of beautifulness, light shining brightly as I enter in

A place with no more worries, heartache, hurt or sin

Don't cry for me I'm with my Father

Free from pain

Free from sorrow

I don't have to wait for a better tomorrow

Don't cry for me I'm with my Father

I'm only a whisper away

You will see me again one day

So hold my smile deeply in your heart

And know that our love will never part

Don't cry for me I'm with my Father

His plan is always divine

He makes no mistakes it was just my time

Don't cry for me I'm with my Father

Gently grabbed my hand

As he led me to his Holy land

Don't cry for me I'm with my Father

Dope Love
(for my honey Rob)

Boy....I'm feeling your vibes

High as a kite completely mesmerized

The connection is real

I can't refute how I feel

You have me spent.....

From the moment our eyes met

You made me regret

All the time lost before

It's hard to ignore

Sugar, you are the one....

Penetrating thoughts of you and I

Bubbling in my soul...

A magic potion of liquid gold

So melodic, exotic, erotic

We have that Dope Love

Grandma's Biscuits

(dedicated to my grandma Catherine)

Nothing compares to my grandma's biscuits

They were oh-so buttery and simply delicious

She would place them on the kitchen table

Ready to demolish and I was more than able!

She made them from scratch

With love and wisdom in every batch

Perfected handcrafted works of art

Sifted... kneaded and straight and from the heart

I sure do miss those biscuits and my grandma dearly

I think about the goodness of them both yearly

Most of all I long for the special times that were spent

With a woman of virtue

A true heaven sent

She was the matriarch of my family

A queen to us all

And if ever we needed advice

We could give her a call

I cherish those memories and hold them close

I miss my grandma's biscuits

But I miss her the most

"Free as a bird to settle where I will." - William Wordsworth

Soar Red Bird Soar

(for my little free spirit Josiah)

The red bird soars high

Whistling cheerful melodies

Gazing over the horizon

Taking in the sweet sound of whispering meadows

His fiery presence calls attention

Demanding the spirit of love and peace

Nestled in the land below

The crisp autumn wind

Rustles shiny feathers as

He glides in and out of fluffy clouds

Soar red bird soar..................

Strong/ powerful/confident

High above for all to see

Gracefully and freely into dawns day

Joy

Joy met me with open arms

    She understood the road traveled

Unlike pain.... joy was pleasant

    She wiped away tears and exuberated my inner being

In her eyes I saw courage

    A strength that only she could give

Her smile ignited all that was dim

    Gave me hope and peace

Allowed me to reach beyond my faults and embrace self

    With joy came... love and understanding

We walked side by side

    I no longer felt alone

Over the hills and through the valley

    She held my hand firmly and never let go

Soul Dance

The thunderous sound of the djembe drum

Sent warm vibrations through feeble bones

Bounced off eardrums and...

 Aroused every fiber of his being

Shackle free

Red earth beneath his feet

He begin to dance

Pulsating and gyrating with great valor

He was no longer a slave to society

Oppression and depression were a thing of the past

His soul was liberated

He exhaled...

Leaving his earthly shell behind

For the first time he felt alive/ebullient

He smiled and began to dance to the beat of his own drum

My flesh and my heart faileth: but God is the strength of my heart, and my portion for ever. Psalms 73:26 (KJV)

But God...

I could've been dead and gone

　Left all alone

But God...

Hurt and abused

Lost and confused

But God...

Deeply depressed

A crazy mess

But God...

Without hope

Strung out on dope

But God...

In the streets

Without food to eat

But God...

He provided a way

Each and everyday

Picked me up when I was down

Turned my situation all around

Wiped away tears

Erased my darkest fears

Patched a heart that was scorned

Was a comfort in the mist of my storm

No one else could have done it.....

But God!

The Grass

Be careful of what you ask for

It may come with so much more

Just because it's appears lush, well-kept, tall and green

There could be dangers lurking, hidden and unseen

When you take that stride

Over to the other side

You may discover that

The grass is not always greener

And ye shall know the truth, and the truth shall make you free.
John 8:32 (KJV)

Stand in Your Truth

Stand in your truth

  Be authentically you

    Each and everyday

      Hold it close and never let it stray

        Shout it out to the masses

          Hang it up on display

            Breathe it

              Speak it

                Live it

                  Own it

                    Regardless of how difficult it may be

                  Your truth embodies power

                Love and integrity

                Stand in your truth

                  It's the only thing that will

                Set you free

About The Author

Tonya is a wife, mother, poet, creative artist, entrepreneur, and community activist. She has worked with diverse economic, social and cultural populations and has a passion for helping others and improving health in underserved and rural communities. She holds a Bachelor of Science degree in Community and Justice Studies from Guilford College and a Master of Arts degree in Human Services Counseling from Liberty University. She currently works in medical education for a large health system. In the 1990's, her interest in writing poetry was sparked when her high school teacher charged her to recite a Maya Angelou poem. Tonya enjoys writing poetry, spending time with family and friends, crafting, music, and reading in her spare time. She is the owner and operator of Tee's Art Expressions where her creativity flows in the form of art, handmade jewelry, handbags, and other accessories.

Tonya resides with family in High Point, North Carolina.

"Love is the only reality and it is not a mere sentiment. It is the ultimate truth that lies at the heart of creation."

Rabindranath Tagore

www.ingramcontent.com/pod-product-compliance
Lightning Source LLC
Chambersburg PA
CBHW062203100526
44589CB00014B/1939